'Hallo! A great deal of steam!
The pudding was out of the copper.
A smell like a washing-day!
That was the cloth. A smell like
an eating-house and a pastrycook's
next door to each other, with a
laundress's next door to that.
That was the pudding.'

Charles Dickens (1812-70), *A Christmas Carol*

VICTORIAN COOKERY

Recipes & History

by
Maggie Black

with a Foreword by
Loyd Grossman OBE

ENGLISH HERITAGE

Front cover: Detail from *Lunchtime Preparations* by William K Blacklock (1872–1924)

Endpapers: Tinplated kitchen equipment. *Left to right:* cake mould, bun tin, biscuit cutter, game pie mould, pastry cutter, biscuit cutter

Published by English Heritage, 23 Savile Row, London W1S 2ET

Copyright © English Heritage and Maggie Black
First published 1985
Revised edition 2004

ISBN 1 85074 873 X

Product code 50853

Edited by Susan Kelleher, Publishing, English Heritage, Kemble Drive, Swindon SN2 2GZ
Designed by Pauline Hull
Picture research by Elaine Willis
Brought to press by Andrew McLaren
Printed in England by CPI Bath

CONTENTS

FOREWORD

Would the pyramids have been built without the recently invented bread to efficiently feed the workforce? Food is a common denominator between us all, and a potent link with our ancestors, just as much as an ancient parish church or a listed house.

I am delighted to contribute a Foreword to English Heritage's series of historic cookery books, which neatly combine two of my passions – history and food. Most of us no longer have to catch or grow our own food before eating it, but the continuing daily need for sustenance still powerfully links us with our earliest forebears. We may not like the thought of Roman fish sauce made from fermented entrails (until we next add oyster sauce to a Chinese beef dish), but we can only sigh with recognition at a Jacobean wife's exhortation to 'let yor butter bee scalding hott in yor pan' before pouring in the beaten eggs for an omelette. The Roman penchant for dormice cooked in milk doesn't resonate with us now, but a dish of pears in red wine features at modern dinner parties just as it did in medieval times.

Food and cooking have inevitably changed down the centuries, as modern cookers have supplanted open hearths, and increased wealth and speedy transport have opened up modern tastes and palates to the widest range of ingredients and cuisines. But it's worth remembering that it was the Romans who gave us onions, sugar was an expensive luxury in the 16th century as was tea in the 17th, the tomato only became popular in Europe in the 19th century and even in the 1950s avocados and red peppers were still exotic foreign imports.

I urge you to experiment with the recipes in these books which cover over 2,000 years, and hope you enjoy, as I have, all that is sometimes strange and often familiar about the taste of times past.

Loyd Grossman OBE
Former Commissioner of English Heritage
Chairman of the Campaign for Museums

INTRODUCTION

Queen Victoria reigned for more than 60 years after succeeding to the throne in 1837 at the age of 18. Her life, spanning most of the 19th century, saw enormous developments both politically and socially. It was an era in which great changes were made to the way in which food was prepared and eaten, and in the variety available.

The foods which ordinary people ate at the beginning of the 19th century were virtually limited to what they could get locally at the time, or what they had preserved at home by pickling, smoking or making into sweet preserves. Almost all essential foodstuffs were still grown or raised on farmland and sold in local markets as transport was difficult. The roads were slow and sometimes dangerous, and there were no railways yet. Only London, a few other city ports, and towns on a navigable river or canal could get supplies from other parts of Britain or overseas.

Since most people still depended on local supplies for staple foods, especially grain, prices varied greatly from place to place. If the harvest failed in the north, corn was scarce and expensive there, even if a good harvest had made it cheap further south.

Bread was everyone's staple food. From about 1800, wheat largely replaced other grains for bread-making, and so became the basic vital commodity. It had to be bought, from abroad if necessary, and milled when needed because the flour was perishable as it still contained the wheatgerm later removed from white flour. Even the whitest and most expensive bread was yellowish and bun-like in consistency because of this.

Descriptions of Jane Austen's home life provide a good idea of what middle-class people ate at the beginning of the 19th century. Her father was a modest country clergyman, fairly typical of his class. He farmed enough land to grow wheat for home bread-making, and kept cows, pigs and sheep for mutton, a favourite standard joint. Lamb at that time meant baby lamb, a delicate dinner-party meat. Mrs Austen kept poultry. She had a varied vegetable garden and fruit trees, and taught

Gloucestershire Old Spot pigs

Opposite: Bread was the nation's staple food in Victorian Britain

her daughters to supervise their maids in making butter and cheese, preserves, pickles and homemade wines, and in brewing beer and curing bacons and hams. The only foods she had to buy were game and fish, and imported goods such as tea, coffee and sugar. When they moved into the town, prices loomed much larger in the family's thinking, and the cost of meat, especially, seemed frighteningly high. But they still ate well, if more simply than their grand neighbours.

The rich lived lavishly, catered for by French-trained chefs, although the only differences between the products that they and their lesser country neighbours ate and drank were that they had various costly luxuries and more imported foods and wines. Despite the war with France which lasted until 1815, the wealthy, who profited from the high wartime prices, could well afford to pay for smuggled wines, tea and sweetmeats. They could also afford exotic foods brought in with the imported staples: sugar, tea, coffee and rice.

For the poor, things were very different. Many country labourers had lost their small homes and vegetable plots as a result of the 18th-century enclosing of land. They were now reduced almost to paupers by having to buy food at wartime prices. Yet peace brought them no relief. The farmers persuaded the government to keep the price of corn (and therefore bread) high. Wages did not rise but unemployment did. Bad harvests followed and there were widespread food riots. In desperation, thousands of men with wives and children, trekked to the squalid slums of the growing cities to work in the factories being set up. A rural cottager who kept his job might still afford a bit of bacon on Sundays, although on other days his family lived largely on bread with a little flavoured lard and potatoes. In the cities, bread and potatoes or porridge were almost the only foods of slum-dwellers. Strong tea, giving an illusion of warmth and fullness, was the main comfort of both urban and rural poor.

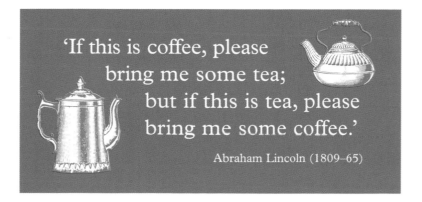

'If this is coffee, please bring me some tea; but if this is tea, please bring me some coffee.'

Abraham Lincoln (1809–65)

Alexis Soyer (1809–58) was renowned for his philanthropy as much as his cooking. Not only did he establish soup kitchens to help the poor, but he also helped feed the troops fighting in the Crimean War. After *The Times* published an open letter from a soldier complaining about the food rations and appealing for his help, Soyer travelled to Scutari to inspect the cooking arrangements. He was horrified at what he saw and soon provided better cooking methods as well as developing a mobile cooking stove. Shaped like a vast dustbin, these stoves were an instant success and have proved

so valuable that they have been used ever since. The Soyer stove, now powered by bottled gas, has been used by the army right up to the present day.

Alexis Soyer (standing with his hands in his pockets) demonstrates his new stoves to Lord Rokeby and General Pelissier in the Crimea, 1855

By the time Victoria came to the throne in 1837, things had gone from bad to worse for the poorer classes because wages fell. In contrast, the middle classes, especially the growing numbers in the cities, were prospering. The new cheap labour pool there was helping to create an industrial and commercial boom – in new food industries among others. The development of macadamised roads and long-distance railways made it possible to transport factory-made and processed goods in bulk quickly and easily. The gap between even the modestly well-paid and the workers widened.

By 1845 the situation was desperate. The poor corn harvest and the falling wage levels added to the misery of the poor. The potato fungus brought famine and starvation to Ireland and to parts of Scotland and England where potatoes now were the main or only food of the poor. The government was forced, at last, to bring down the price of bread.

The famine also brought home to some of the better-off how many of the working people they called 'the poor' were actually destitute, and made them want to do something for the starving. For instance, two renowned London chefs, Alexis Soyer and Charles Francatelli, more used to handling delicacies such as ortolans and truffles, designed new soup recipes for cheap mass feeding. The soups had little nourishment value, but the gesture marked the start of a new humanitarian movement.

After 1848, the variety, quality and freshness of food in the cities began to improve for everyone, mainly because the railways distributed fresh foods, such as milk, and the new, bulk-processed foods efficiently and quickly.

The urban middle classes benefited most. They were becoming more and more prosperous and conscious of their rising social status. They ate well to show it off, and since they did not grow or preserve their own food, they bought the new, better quality meat and vegetables, and the mass-produced and mass-preserved foods which now came into the shops.

However, poor people also began to eat slightly better. By 1864 a country labourer with a job could afford one hot meal a week and some vegetables. Better-off artisans might have a cheap knuckle joint now and then cooked at the baker's, or get a midday meal of meat and root vegetables, bread, cheese and beer at a tavern or basement cookshop.

Even the poor who still subsisted mostly on bread and potatoes were catered for by manufacturers and importers of the cheapest new mass-market foods. For instance, when cattle disease sent meat prices sky-high in 1865, importers bought in cheap, fatty American bacon and Australian canned meats. Poor folk could also now get cheap, dark treacle to flavour their bread. Then, towards the end of the 19th century, cheap jam made of coloured, sweetened vegetables or fruit pulp offered them a sweeter, if less nourishing, alternative.

> 'The rule is jam tomorrow and jam yesterday, but never jam today.'
>
> Lewis Carroll (Charles Lutwidge Dodgson) (1819–80)

The poor benefited from another development. In 1861, roller mills came into use in Britain, and by the 1870s gave everyone refined white flour without wheatgerm.

However, most of the new processed, packeted, bottled and canned foods which came in during the second half of the 19th century were only for people who lived 'above stairs'. The poor could neither afford them nor make use of them.

Those foods were legion: it would be impossible to list them all. Here are some which changed the look and taste of the dishes on middle-class tables:

Quick-acting compressed yeast, self-raising flour, baking powder.
These changed bread and cake-making recipes a great deal.

Custard powder, blancmange powder and concentrated egg powder.

Bottled, gelatine-based jellies, and later, stiffer table jellies in packets.
These let housewives with little time and money make elaborate desserts like those of the wealthy.

Bulk-produced cheese made in factories. This replaced farm cheese.

Sweetened condensed milk, dried milk.

Margarine (at first made from beef and milk). It was cheap, although it tasted oily and insipid to begin with.

 Bulk-dried vegetables and dried packeted soups.

Commercially bottled pickles and sauces. Some, such as the products of Harry J Heinz, had a novelty value at first but soon became household names.

An advertisement for Heinz tomato soup from about 1900

Experiments in bottling and canning meat in bulk had been going on since the beginning of the 19th century in both France and England, not to help the housewife but to feed the troops and sailors. In 1865 the Admiralty set up the first large-scale meat-canning factory. Ten years later canned meats from both Australia

and America were being imported. This marked a significant change – by the end of the 19th century Britain relied on imported food.

Fish supplies to the expanding cities before the 1850s had been insufficient and more than often rotten or tainted. The supply improved rapidly when steam trawlers replaced the old sailing boats, and the invention of trawling made cod an everyday fish instead of a luxury one. As the railways spread and speeded up, fish even reached inland towns safely in ice imported in bulk from Iceland and Norway. The ice-man who brought a great dripping block of ice to a well-to-do Victorian home before a dinner party became a familiar sight. However, another familiar sight now disappeared. The oyster stalls in the poor quarters of London had to close down as in about 1850, the oysters which had been a staple food for the very poor, became an almost unobtainable luxury due to over-fishing and pollution.

Chilling or freezing meat in bulk was not practical until a cheap way of making ice was found in 1861. Even then, it took until 1880 to find a way of refrigerating and transporting bulk meat in good condition; so chilled and frozen meat became a major source of supply only at the end of the century.

By the end of the Victorian era, the cook's store cupboard and larder in the middle-class city home of the 1890s were as full of packets and cans as any modern kitchen. With the help of bottled sauces, canned vegetables and fruit, and essences, she could choose between as many flavours (if less subtle ones) as a skilled chef who still made all the kitchen 'basics' by hand.

'The food of thy soul is light and space; feed it then on light and space. But the food of thy body is champagne and oysters; feed it then on champagne and oysters; and so shall it merit a joyful resurrection, if there is any to be.'

Herman Melville (1819–91)

Most fresh foods came to her door. The baker and muffin-man called daily. The fishmonger with his ice-laden cart brought cod, hake, salmon, skate, eels, herrings and shellfish; even lobsters were still a reasonable price. She could buy most vegetables in

season from the greengrocer's cart, from asparagus in spring to pumpkin at Hallowe'en, although she would have to prepare all her vegetables and her fish herself. The milkman would still fill her jug with milk or cream from his churn; bottling and pasteurisation did not come in until the 1920s. However, railway transport from the country, machine milking and cooking gave her cleaner milk than before 1860 – although she would still be wise not to look too closely at its blueish tint.

She would really only have to leave her basement kitchen to visit the butcher and poulterer. Veal was still the cheapest meat to use for everyday meals and white stock; the family would not despise a well-dressed calf's head, and the feet still made the best reputed jelly. Mutton had gone down a little in the social scale; Irish stew was now made from scrag and was a servants' dish, although a roasted joint looked handsome on the dinner table. A fine chicken or capon was as much a

An illustration from Mrs Beeton's *Every Day Cookery* showing useful varieties of game

Mrs Lockey	12	
Head Laundry Maid	6	
2nd Do Do	5	5
Head Housemaid	7	0
2nd Do	5	0
3rd Do	4	0
4 Do	3	0
Kitchen Maid	6	0
Scullery Maid	4	0
Still Room Maid		
House Keeper	12	0
One Month Beer & Washing		
from Nov to Dec 1st		
4 Housemaids	3	

party dish as a pheasant. Small birds such as woodcock and snipe were popular savouries.

Amongst the working class, some poorer slum children still had only bread and jam, or porridge for seventeen out of twenty-one meals in the week, and there were many waifs who got less. But there was a strong humanitarian movement now to help the needy. Well-meaning people produced dozens of cookbooks aimed at teaching the poor how to use their small resources well – although these were not as a rule very practical because few ordinary people knew anything about nutrition yet, or the real problems involved.

In the country, conditions and wages varied, and in some parts, labourers and their families did not get enough to eat. On the other hand, many farmers gave their workers food 'perks', or let them 'buy' food by doing overtime, and most still let women and children into the fields to glean after the harvest. Children got off school to go nutting in season, or to pick field mushrooms.

This was at the lowest end of the social scale. There were many grades of working people, and some (such as skilled craftsmen or the upper servants in a big house) now lived almost as well as their employers.

Opposite: A page from an accounts book at Brodsworth Hall which lists the wages paid to servants

Recipes

DINNER-PARTY DISHES

POULET SAUTÉ À LA PLOMBIÈRE

A decorative hot entrée for a formal dinner in 1895 which would make a practical main dish by itself today.

2 small chickens, about 900 g
    (2 lb) each
100 g (4 oz) streaky bacon
50 g (2 oz) unsalted butter
2 shallots, finely chopped
15 ml (1 tbls) flour
15 ml (1 tbls) mild curry powder
10 ml (2 tsps) desiccated
    coconut
125 ml (4 fl oz) white wine
15 ml (1 tbls) brandy
575 ml (1 pt) white stock
4 parsley sprigs and 1/2 bay leaf,
    tied in muslin

salt and pepper
a pinch of grated nutmeg
5 ml (1 tsp) redcurrant jelly
juice of 1/2 sour orange
175 g (6 oz) long grain rice
a little extra stock (optional)

To garnish:
rind of 1/2 orange, pared thinly
    and cut into matchsticks
6–8 warm fleurons (half-moons)
    of cooked puff pastry

Joint the chickens and dice the bacon, discarding any rind. Melt the butter in a saucepan or flameproof casserole. Fry the bacon for about 2 minutes, shaking the pan, then add the chicken pieces and shallots, and sauté until lightly browned on all sides. Mix together the flour, curry powder and coconut and sprinkle over the chicken. Stir round, and pour in the wine, brandy and stock. Add the herb bundle, then bring to the boil and add the seasoning, nutmeg, redcurrant jelly and orange juice. Reduce the heat and simmer, uncovered, for 30 minutes or until the chicken pieces are tender. While the meat is simmering, cook the rice in boiling, salted water until tender, then drain and keep warm. Skim off any fat from the curry sauce, remove the herb bundle, and thin with a little extra stock if wished. Simmer the shreds of orange rind in water for 2 minutes and then drain. Arrange the rice in a circle, pile the chicken, bacon and sauce in the centre, and garnish the top with shreds of rind and warmed fleurons.

Charles Herman Senn: *Recherché Cookery*

'Oh, the tiger will love you. There is no sincerer love than the love of food.'

George Bernard Shaw (1856–1950)

RICE À LA SOEUR NIGHTINGALE
(Sister Nightingale's Rice)

175 g (6 oz) long grain rice
salt and pepper
450 g (1 lb) smoked haddock fillet
2 square slices bread, crusts
   removed
75–100 g (3–4 oz) unsalted butter
3 hard-boiled eggs
a pinch of grated nutmeg
15 ml (1 tbls) Parmesan cheese,
   grated

Cook the rice in plenty of boiling, salted water until tender. While the rice is cooking, pour boiling water over the haddock, and leave to stand for 5 minutes. Drain the rice when ready. Cut each bread slice into four triangles. Fry in 40 g (1½ oz) of the butter until golden on both sides. Remove with a fish slice, leaving any fat in the pan.

Drain on absorbent paper, then keep warm. Separate the whites and yolks of the hard-boiled eggs into separate bowls. Chop the whites. Remove any bones and skin from the fish and flake the flesh coarsely. Mix with the chopped egg whites. Add the remaining butter to the frying pan and toss the rice in it over a gentle heat, adding seasoning and nutmeg to taste. Mix in the fish and egg white mixture, and pile in a pyramid on a hot dish. Sieve the egg yolks and cheese together, and sprinkle over the mixture. Put in the oven at gas mark 4, 180°C (350°F) for 4–5 minutes until the cheese begins to colour. Add the triangles of fried bread and serve at once.

Charles Elmé Francatelli: *The Cook's Guide*
and Housekeeper's and Butler's Assistant

WHITE SOUP À LA REINE

This was a popular cream soup offered at affluent dinner parties throughout the period. Notice that the stock is made with veal. Calves were slaughtered early, and the meat was plentiful and cheap.

1 chicken, cooked
1.7 l (3 pt) water
450 g (1 lb) veal, cubed
1 carrot
1 stick celery
1 onion
350 g (12 oz) rice
1.7 l (3 pt) veal or chicken stock
25 g (1 oz) butter
salt and pepper
275 ml (¹/₂ pt) single cream

To serve:

croutons

Remove the meat from the cooked chicken and set aside. Put the carcass in a saucepan, add the water, veal, carrot, celery and onion and simmer for about 2 hours to make a broth. Strain. Meanwhile, simmer the rice very gently in the veal or chicken stock for about 40 minutes until all the stock is absorbed. Work the chicken meat in a food processor with the butter and 150 ml (¹/₄ pt) of the broth. When it is reduced to a smooth pulp, add the rice and work into the mixture. Mix with 1.1 l (2 pt) of the broth, then strain the soup through a nylon sieve lined with cheesecloth. Heat the strained soup in a saucepan, season to taste, then stir in the cream. Serve with croutons on the top.

Charles Elmé Francatelli: *The Cook's Guide and Housekeeper's and Butler's Assistant*

CALF'S FOOT JELLY

Chefs and good cooks still considered it necessary to make calf's foot jelly, not only as nourishment for invalids, but as by far and away the best basis for their many (often elaborate) jellied desserts. Isinglass was accepted as an alternative but was less esteemed. Gelatine, made by boiling hooves and hides, came into its own when the first cheap jellies became an 'instant' success at the Great Exhibition of 1851, but made any high-class cook wince.

To make 'jelly stock': 'Take two calfs' feet, cut them up and boil in three quarts of water; as soon as it boils remove it to the corner of the fire, and simmer for five hours, keeping it skimmed, pass through a hair sieve into a basin, and let it remain until quite hard, then remove the oil and fat, and wipe the top dry. Place in a stewpan one gill of water, one of sherry, half a pound of lump sugar, the juice of four lemons, the rinds of two, and the whites and shells of five eggs, whisk until the sugar is melted, then add the jelly, place it on the fire, and whisk until boiling, pass it through a jelly-bag, pouring that back again which comes through first until quite clear; it is then ready for use, by putting it in moulds or glasses.'

Alexis Soyer:
The Modern Housewife or Ménagère

29

MACARONI À LA REINE

Miss Acton's 'excellent and delicate mode of dressing macaroni' makes delightful reading but long-winded instruction. Its essentials in modern terms are these.

225 g (8 oz) macaroni
275 g (10 oz) white Stilton or
  other rich white quick-melting
  cheese without rind (see note)
50 g (2 oz) unsalted butter
350 ml (12 fl oz) double cream
  or thick rich white sauce
salt and pepper
a good pinch of ground mace
a pinch of cayenne pepper
fried breadcrumbs, finely
  crushed

Cook the macaroni in boiling salted water until tender, then drain. While it is cooking, flake the cheese and the butter. Heat the cream or sauce almost to boiling point. Add the cheese and butter in small portions, with salt, pepper, mace and cayenne, and stir until dissolved. Pour over the hot, drained macaroni, and toss to mix. Turn into a warmed serving dish, and sprinkle thickly with golden crumbs before serving.

Eliza Acton: *Modern Cookery for Private Families*, 1874 edition

Miss Acton suggests using Stilton without the blue mould. Perhaps young Stiltons were less blued in those days.

PHEASANT GITANA

Weekend shooting and house parties were a feature of upper-class Victorian life. This was a useful way to handle a badly-shot bird for formal dining.

1 pheasant, trussed
225 g (8 oz) streaky bacon, rinded and cut into 2.5 cm (1 in) squares
25 g (1 oz) butter
1 garlic clove
2 large Spanish onions, sliced
4 ripe tomatoes, sliced
150 ml (¹/₄ pt) sherry
5 ml (1 tsp) paprika

Put the pheasant in a large flameproof casserole with the bacon, butter and garlic. Fry, turning the pheasant, until it is browned all over. Pour off excess fat, then add the onions, tomatoes and sherry. Cover and simmer for 45–60 minutes until the pheasant is tender, shaking the pan occasionally. Just before serving, stir in the paprika.

Charles Elmé Francatelli: *The Cook's Guide and Housekeeper's and Butler's Assistant*

Gertie Gitana was a popular star of Victorian music halls.

Opposite: The result of a shooting party at Brodsworth Hall

32

SAVOY CAKE

A grand dinner party or banquet always featured large and small cakes, especially Savoy cake, among its sweet entremets or desserts. Since stale Savoy cake was also the basis of creamy desserts such as Coburg pudding and trifle, a shrewd chef included these in his menu too. This is Alexis Soyer's basic Savoy cake, probably made, as was common, in a fancy mould rather like a jelly mould. Hot steamed and similar puddings were also made in fancy moulds so that they looked elaborately carved when turned out.

clarified butter
225 g (8 oz) caster sugar, plus a little extra
1–2 drops lemon essence

7 eggs, separated
75 g (3 oz) plain flour
75 g (3 oz) potato flour

Brush the inside of a 2.5 l (4½ pt) decorative mould or a 20 cm (8 in) diameter, 7.5 cm (3 in) deep cake tin with clarified butter. Invert it to drain. When the butter has set, sprinkle the inside of the mould or tin liberally with caster sugar, and shake out the excess. Add the lemon essence to the caster sugar, then beat with the egg yolks in a large bowl until thick and almost white. Separately, whisk the egg whites until stiff but not dry. Mix the plain and potato flour and sift a little into the egg yolk mixture, folding it in with a metal spoon. Fold in about half the egg whites, then sift and fold in about half the remaining flour mixture. Repeat, using all the ingredients. Using a spatula, turn the mixture into the prepared mould or tin as lightly as possible. Bake at gas mark 4, 180°C (350°F) for 1–1¼ hours. Test for readiness by running a hot thin skewer into the cake. Turn out to cool on a wire rack. (Leave for 1–2 days before cutting up to make into a dessert.)

Alexis Soyer:
The Modern Housewife or Ménagère

Herman Senn, a well-known Victorian chef, baked this quantity of Savoy cake mixture in a large ring mould. When it was cold, he filled the centre with a good half-pint of vanilla-flavoured, sweetened whipped cream, and titled it 'Gateau de Savoie à la Chantilly'. International menu French had become 'the thing' for even middle-class formal dinners by this time. Perhaps that was why he called his big cookbook of 1893 *Practical Gastronomy and Culinary Dictionary: A Complete Menu Compiler and Register of Most Known Dishes in English and French.*

ICED PUDDINGS

One or more elaborately moulded iced puddings were served at any formal Victorian dinner or banquet. This description of how to freeze an ice-cream pudding was written by Samuel Hobbs, a freelance chef who prepared many dinners for royalty. His puddings were made with about 1.2 l (2¼ pt) cream custard and were meant for 14 people, a fairly small number for a Victorian dinner party.

'...freeze the pudding as follows: place the same in a three-quart pewter freezer; break up or pound as fine as possible twenty pounds of rough ice and put the cover on your freezer; mix three or four double handfuls of fine salt with the pounded ice well and rapidly together; place the same round the freezer in a tub or pail and by holding the handle, turn the freezer round and round for about ten minutes; then take off the lid of the freezer and with the ice spatula, remove the pudding which you will find has frozen to the side of the freezer and mix the same with the unfrozen part of the pudding; now put on the lid and proceed again as in the first instance ...

A Victorian wooden ice-cream maker

again remove the lid and mix the frozen with the unfrozen part … till it becomes smooth and uniform in appearance. You should now turn the freezer by the aid of your spatula, beating the pudding with the same, so as to make the freezer spin round; this should be continued till the pudding is sufficiently frozen and by this process becomes very smooth and firm …
Then fill your pudding mould as follows: remove the freezer from the ice and scoop the remainder of the ice into a pail, mix fresh salt with the same as before, and then with your spatula, or a spoon, fill the ice pudding mould with the frozen pudding, tapping the same so that the pudding will, when turned out of the mould, show smooth and compact. The pudding should be well embedded in ice, under and over it;

and if more ice is needed, proceed to prepare as in the first instance; let the pudding remain in this till required for dinner, when remove the mould from the ice and dip it into a pail of water, slightly warm; then dry it in a cloth, remove the lid, also the bottom of the mould, and the pudding with a little shake will leave the mould and fix itself on to the silver dish upon which it should be sent to table.'

Samuel Hobbs: *One Hundred and Sixty Culinary Dainties for the Epicure, the Invalid and the Dyspeptic*

A modern ice-cream maker should produce the same effect as a Victorian churn freezer, although the ice-cream quantities will have to be adapted to fit its smaller capacity.

PETITES BOUCHÉES

These little pastries were offered among Victorian sweet entremets or desserts at formal dinners and evening parties.

175 g (6 oz) whole almonds
100 g (4 oz) caster sugar
rind of ¹/₂ lemon, pared thinly
I egg white
275 g (10 oz) puff pastry

Blanch the almonds by plunging them in boiling water for about 3 minutes, then rub off the skins and chop very finely. Pound together the sugar and lemon rind in a mortar, then sift to remove any solid rind. Mix in the almonds. Beat the egg white until liquid, and mix into the almonds and sugar to make a paste (you may not need it all). Roll out the puff pastry to a thickness of 5 mm (¹/₄ in) and cut into diamonds, rounds, ovals, etc. Re-roll and recut trimmings. Spread the pastry shapes thickly with the almond paste. Bake at gas mark 6, 200°C (400°F) until gilded. Cool on a wire rack.

Mrs Isabella Beeton:
The Book of Household Management, 1866

Opposite: A selection of tempting desserts from Mrs Beeton's recipes

Tartlets.

Mince Pies.

Vanilla Cream.

e Marmalade Tart

Cherry Tart.

Pear & Apple Dumplings.

Charlotte Russe.

Dessert Biscuits.

Gingerbread Pudding.

Fruit Tart.

Milk Pudding

Christmas Plum Pudding.

Apples & Rice.

Pancakes.

BAVARIAN CREAMS

Soyer, in The Modern Housewife, *explains how these 'creams' can be flavoured like jellies with ripe fruit in syrup or preserves. He gives a basic recipe for a plain one, using generous Victorian quantities. It has been adapted for modern use.*

1 vanilla pod, split
575 ml (1 pt) milk
5 egg yolks
175 g (6 oz) caster sugar
45 ml (3 tbls) any sweet liqueur
25 g (1 oz) gelatine
425 ml (3/4 pt) whipping cream

Simmer the vanilla pod in the milk for 10 minutes. Meanwhile, beat the egg yolks and sugar together in a saucepan until thick and quite white. Still beating, add the hot milk gradually and place over a low heat until the custard thickens. Strain into a bowl and cool. While cooling, heat the liqueur in a small pan until very hot; sprinkle in the gelatine little by little and stir until it dissolves. Do not allow to boil. Stir it into the cooling custard and chill until the mixture begins to thicken up at the edges. While chilling, whip the cream fairly stiffly. Fold it into the thickening custard. Pour into a wetted 1.7 l (3 pt) ornamental mould and leave for at least 2 hours. Turn out on to a chilled serving dish.

Alexis Soyer: *The Modern Housewife or Ménagère*

CHARLOTTE RUSSE

This is one of Soyer's recipes using the previous recipe.

'Line the inside of a plain round mould with Savoy biscuits, cutting and placing them at the bottom to form a rosette, standing them upright and close together [round the sides] … fill with any [liqueur-flavoured] cream, place the mould in ice, let it remain until ready to serve, turn over on a dish and remove the mould.'

Alexis Soyer: *The Modern Housewife or Ménagère*

Use sponge fingers for the Savoy biscuits.

EVERYDAY DISHES

MOCK CRAB

This version of a Victorian luncheon dish appears in a book by a dour Scots cook. Not all Victorian cookery was rich and showy. Simple as this is, the recipes in Mrs Black's other books were drab by comparison.

1 hard-boiled egg
15 ml (1 tbls) salad oil
2.5 ml (1/2 tsp) salt
2.5 ml (1/2 tsp) caster sugar
2.5 ml (1/2 tsp) made English
    mustard
15 ml (1 tbls) white wine vinegar
a few drops of onion juice
100 g (4 oz) red Cheshire or
    Leicester cheese, coarsely grated

15 ml (1 tbls) cooked chicken,
    finely chopped

To serve:
1 crab shell or lettuce leaves
thin slices of brown bread and
    butter, rolled

Separate the egg yolk and white. Sieve the yolk into a small bowl. Separately, finely chop the white and keep aside for garnishing. Work the sieved yolk to a smooth paste with the oil, using the back of a spoon. Mix in the salt, sugar and mustard, then blend in the vinegar and onion juice to make a thin cream. Mix together the cheese and chicken lightly with a fork, keeping the cheese shreds separate, then blend in the vinegar mixture lightly. Chill. To serve, pile in the crab shell or on lettuce leaves and garnish with the chopped egg white. Serve with rolls of thin bread and butter.

Mrs Black: *Superior Cookery*

BOILED SALAD

'Take Beetroot. Boil it well and slice it neatly. Take Celery. Boil it well and cut it in large pieces. Some slices of Potato, also boiled and neatly cut. Some Brussels Sprouts are sometimes added. Add a rich Salad Sauce, composed of cream, Eggs, and mustard. To be eaten cold. Like a Lobster salad – to which dish it bears a very great outward resemblance.'

Janey Ellice's Recipes 1846–1859

The cheeseboard provided a fitting end to a fine meal, but cheese was also used a great deal in recipes such as Mock Crab

STEWED TROUT

A 19th-century cook had no frozen, farmed and supermarket trout, only river fish which might be much larger if old and wily. The cooking time below has been adapted to suit both; otherwise the author's tasty recipe is almost unchanged.

2 medium-sized trout
75 g (3 oz) butter
15 ml (1 tbls) flour
a good pinch of ground mace
a good pinch of grated nutmeg
a pinch of cayenne pepper
425 ml (³/4 pt) veal or chicken stock
3 parsley sprigs
1 bay leaf
1 broad strip lemon peel, rolled
salt
30 ml (2 tbls) dry white wine
(optional)

Clean the fish, and trim the tails and fins; remove heads if you wish. Rinse inside and pat quite dry. Melt the butter in a large deep frying pan or skillet. Stir in the flour, mace, nutmeg and cayenne together. Add the trout, and brown them on both sides, shaking the pan to prevent them sticking. Now add the stock, parsley, bay leaf, lemon peel, salt and wine if using. Half-cover the pan, and reduce the heat to a gentle simmer. Cook for 15–35 minutes depending on the size of the fish. When ready, the fish should be tender when pierced with a thin skewer, but not soft enough to break up. Remove the fish to a warmed serving dish. Skim all the fat off the cooking liquid, and strain some or all of it over the fish. Serve at once.

Eliza Acton: *Modern Cookery for Private Families*

HODGE PODGE

This is Mrs Beeton's recipe for leftovers from stewed well-aged spring lamb. Other writers, such as Eliza Acton, had made it with raw meat and called it China chilo. From the mid-19th century, even great chefs granted that most people sometimes ate leftovers. In 1853, Alexis Soyer called his similar dish simply 'Remains'. Even thriftier than Mrs Beeton, he suggested using leftover peas and other vegetables served with the original roast.

**450 g (1 lb) lightly cooked lamb
  or mutton
225 g (8 oz) firm-hearted lettuce
6 spring onions
50 g (2 oz) butter or margarine
salt and pepper
100 ml (4 fl oz) water
275 g (10 oz) shelled garden peas**

Mince the meat coarsely, discarding skin and excess fat. Slice the lettuce and spring onions and put them in a saucepan with the meat. Add the fat, and season generously. Pour the water over the dish. Cover, and simmer gently for 45 minutes. Meanwhile, boil the peas for about 5 minutes or until just tender. Drain and add them to the meat just before serving. (Cooked peas can be added to the meat a few minutes before the end of the cooking time.) By then, the liquid in the pan should almost all have been absorbed.

Mrs Isabella Beeton:
The Book of Household Management

This dish is much better flavoured if, like Eliza Acton's China chilo, it contains a large, finely chopped onion, and 10 ml (2 tsps) of curry powder.

DORMERS

Between dinner parties, much Victorian cookery was in the boiled cod and cabbage class to make up for the cost of the parties. These 'sausages' were probably eaten as a supper dish, but would be good for breakfast or as part of a mixed grill with bacon instead of gravy.

225 g (8oz) cold cooked lamb or mutton, without skin or bone
75 g (3 oz) cold cooked rice
50 g (2 oz) shredded suet
salt and ground black pepper
1 large egg
25 g (1 oz) fine dried breadcrumbs
dripping or bacon fat for frying
leftover gravy

Chop or mince the meat, rice and suet together fairly finely. Season well. Turn on to a board and divide into six equal-sized portions. Squeeze and shape each portion into a small roll or sausage shape. Beat the egg with a fork on a plate. Scatter the breadcrumbs on a sheet of greaseproof paper. Roll the 'sausages' in beaten egg, coating completely, then cover with crumbs. Leave to stand for 15–30 minutes. Heat the fat in a frying pan, and turn the 'sausages' over in the hot oil until crisp and browned on all sides. Drain on absorbent paper, then place on a warm serving dish. While the 'sausages' are resting, skim the surface of any leftover gravy and dilute it if needed. Bring to simmering point in a small saucepan while frying the 'sausages', then pour the gravy around them just before serving.

Mrs Isabella Beeton:
The Book of Household Management

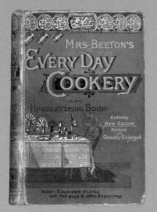

Mrs Beeton is the best known of all Victorian cooks and well over a century later her recipes are still enjoyed all over the world. She was born Isabella Mary Mayson in London on 12 March 1836, the daughter of a linen draper. Her father died when she was very young, and her mother later remarried a widower with four young children. Their combined family of eight eventually became twenty-one!

In July 1856, Isabella married Samuel Orchart Beeton, a publisher who had founded the *Englishwoman's Domestic Magazine* in 1852. Soon after their marriage Isabella began to contribute a cookery column and within a short time she was editing the magazine as well as starting the *Young Englishwoman*, a penny weekly for girls. Her most famous work *Beeton's Book of Household Management* took four years to research in which she personally tried out all the recipes. It was published in 1861 and immediately sold well – and continues to do so. Tragically, Isabella died in 1865 of puerperal fever a week after the birth of her fourth son. She was only 28.

Above: Front cover of Mrs Beeton's *Every Day Cookery and Housekeeping Book*, 1890
Opposite: Mrs Isabella Beeton

49

IRISH STEW

Irish stew seems to have been christened as such only in the early 19th century. At first it was a middle-class dish using loin or best end chops.

900 g (2 lb) neck chops of well-aged lamb or mutton
900 g (2 lb) potatoes, sliced
1 slice of ham, diced (optional)
6 small onions, weighing about 400 g (14 oz), sliced
7.5 ml (1¹/₂ tsps) salt
2.5 ml (¹/₂ tsp) white pepper
10 ml (2 tsps) mushroom ketchup
425 ml (³/₄ pt) stock or leftover gravy

Ask the butcher to cut through any long rib bones. Take them off and use for stock. Place a layer of potatoes in the bottom of a deep flameproof casserole holding about 2.8 litres (5 pints). Cover with chops and a little ham, if using, then with a layer of onions. Sprinkle with seasoning. Repeat the layers until the dish is full, ending with potatoes. Mix the ketchup into the stock or gravy and pour over the dish. Cover tightly, and place over a very low heat. Simmer gently until tender, about 1¹/₂ hours for best end or loin chops, 2–2¹/₂ hours for middle neck or scrag.

William Kitchiner: *The Cook's Oracle*, 1836 edition

Eliza Acton, writing a little later than Dr Kitchiner, omits the ham, makes onions optional, and doubles the quantity of potatoes, which she says should be boiled to a mash.

CAROTTES NOUVELLES À LA FLAMANDE

In formal Victorian menus, vegetables whether used for garnishing or served as a separate course, were almost always sculptured, stuffed or richly sauced – and overcooked.

600 g (1 1/4 lb) young spring carrots
salt and pepper
25 g (1 oz) butter
a pinch of grated nutmeg
2 pinches of caster sugar
7.5 ml (1/2 tbls) flour
275 ml (1/2 pt) white stock
2 egg yolks
65 ml (2 1/2 fl oz) single cream
10 ml (2 tsps) chopped parsley

To garnish:

croutons

Wash and scrape the carrots (they should all be one size if possible). Quarter them neatly and parboil them for 10 minutes in salted water. Drain. Melt the butter in a pan, add the carrots, season with salt, pepper, nutmeg and caster sugar. Sprinkle in the flour and toss over the heat for a few minutes. Add the stock, cover the pan tightly and simmer gently for about 20 minutes, stirring occasionally. When the carrots are soft, beat the egg yolks and cream together then add to the pan, stirring gently until thickened. Pour on to a warm serving dish, sprinkle with parsley and garnish with a few croutons.

Charles Herman Senn: *Practical Gastronomy and Culinary Dictionary*

STEWED OX-KIDNEY

Not what we would call a stew today, but it is still good for its original purpose, as a 'plain entrée or side dish for every-day fare'. Notice that even this top-class chef did not scorn bottled sauces.

450–600 g (1–1¹/₄ lb) ox kidney
45 ml (3 tbls) butter
50 g (2 oz) mushrooms, chopped

10 ml (2 tsps) parsley, chopped
1 shallot, chopped
salt and pepper
15 ml (1 tbls) flour
10 ml (2 tsps) Harvey's sauce
5 ml (1 tsp) lemon juice
150 ml (¹/₄ pt) beef stock or water
very small squares or triangles of dry toast

Harvey's sauce was a popular Victorian condiment. It had been one of the first commercially successful bottled sauces, along with Lazenby's Anchovy Essence; both had been created at the end of the 18th century by innkeeper Peter Harvey and his sister Elizabeth Lazenby.

Skin and core the kidney, and cut it across into thin rounds. Heat 30 ml (2 tbls) of the butter in a frying pan and sear the kidney slices on both sides briefly; they should be pink in the centre. Add the mushrooms, parsley and shallot, and toss in the butter until well coated. Add the remaining butter if needed. Season well, then sprinkle in the flour and stir in the Harvey's sauce and the lemon juice. Add the stock or water slowly, and stir over fairly low heat for 4–5 minutes until the shallot is tender and the sauce is almost reduced to a glaze. Add a little more stock if needed. Arrange the toast triangles or squares around a warmed serving dish with the sauced kidney in the centre.

Charles Elmé Francatelli: *The Cook's Guide and Housekeeper's and Butler's Assistant*

MULLIGATAWNY SOUP
(Pepper Water)

450 g (1 lb) lean lamb or beef
1 small cooking apple
1 onion
50 g (2 oz) butter
30 ml (2 tbls) curry powder
50 g (2 oz) plain flour
1 l (1³/₄ pt) stock
salt and pepper

Cut the meat into small cubes. Peel the apple and onion and chop finely. Melt the butter in a deep saucepan and fry the meat, apple and onion quickly for 2–3 minutes. Add the curry powder, cook gently for 2 minutes, then stir in the flour. Gradually add the stock and seasoning and stir until boiling. Simmer until meat is tender, then strain and serve with long-grain rice.

D'ARTOIS OF APRICOT

Both chefs and domestic cooks gave similar recipes for these popular little pastries; Francatelli's is one of the clearest. The only changes in the recipe below are one or two ideas from Victorian cookbooks, suggesting, for instance, a size for the d'artois.

450 g (1 lb) puff pastry
apricot jam
1 well-beaten egg mixed with a
few drops of water
caster sugar

Take one-third of the pastry, and roll it out on a lightly floured surface into an oblong which will just fit on to a baking sheet about 35x30 cm (14x12 in) in size. You could use a standard 35x25 cm (14x10 in) Swiss roll tin turned upside down. Lay the pastry on the tin. Spread a thick even layer of apricot jam over the pastry to within 2.5 cm (1 in) of the edge. Brush the edge with beaten egg, using a brush dipped in cold water. Roll out the remaining pastry to fit the first sheet. Lay it over it, and press down the edges to seal. With the back of a knife, mark the pastry into small oblongs about 7.5 cm (3 in) long and 2.5 cm (1 in) wide. Brush evenly all over with egg. Using a small knife, flick up tiny nicks of pastry in rows, making a kind of feather pattern on each cake. Bake at gas mark 6, 200°C (400°F) for 15–20 minutes. When risen and golden brown, sprinkle evenly with sugar. Return to the oven for 2–3 minutes to melt it, then place under a moderate grill for a moment or two to glaze. Cool and cut into oblongs.

To serve, arrange a row in a circle on a doily, place another on top, then another until all are arranged.

Charles Elmé Francatelli: *The Cook's Guide and Housekeeper's and Butler's Assistant*

Pastry cream, apple marmalade or any kind of preserve can be used in the d'artois. They are less fragile if made a little wider.

CHARITY FOOD

POOR MEN'S PIES

Victorian reformers and writers were always conscious that the poor needed help, but generally believed that the way to give it was to teach them to make the best use of their small resources. Well-meaning ladies and great chefs alike poured out instructive recipes for the wives of city artisans and rural labourers, assuming that they had the means and facilities to use them, and the time and energy to read and act on them.

Soyer, who pioneered the soup kitchens for the destitute, created a 'Labourer's Pie' with several pounds of meat and long instructions on how to make a well-fitting pastry lid. Here is a more practical pie

where the cost of the ingredients are concerned, although the author's knowledge of nutrition was nil.

75 g (3 oz) tapioca
100 g (4 oz) dripping
225 g (8 oz) onions, sliced
1.6 kg (3½ lb) potatoes, sliced
salt and pepper
225 g (8 oz) flour
5 ml (1 tsp) baking powder

Wash the tapioca and soak for 1 hour in cold water. Take 25 g (1 oz) of the dripping and put a little of it at the bottom of a pie dish. Add some onion, tapioca, potatoes and seasoning. Repeat the layers until the onions, tapioca and potatoes have all been used. Mix the flour, baking powder, some salt and the remaining 75 g (3 oz) dripping, adding enough cold water to make a smooth paste. Roll out and use to make a lid for the pie. Bake at gas mark 6, 200°C (400°F) for about 1 1/4 hours. Serve hot.

Martha H Gordon:
Cookery for Working Men's Wives

A half-penny soup kitchen in London, 1870

POOR MAN'S SOUP

Soyer's soup kitchen meal for the starving was widely publicised and copied. Although only slightly more nourishing than other soup handouts which he condemned, it did a lot to jolt the consciences of the affluent who accepted his flamboyant (and sometimes specious) arguments and appeal to them.

50 g (2 oz) dripping
100 g (4 oz) meat cut into 2.5 cm (1 in) dice
100 g (4 oz) onions, thinly sliced
100 g (4 oz) turnips, cut into small dice ('the peel will do')
75 g (3 oz) celery
50 g (2 oz) leeks, thinly sliced ('the green tops will do')
350 g (12 oz) wholemeal flour
225 g (8 oz) pearl barley

75 g (3 oz) salt
7 g ('/4 oz) brown sugar
9 l (2 gals) water

'I first put two ounces of dripping in a saucepan (capable of holding two gallons of water), with a quarter of a pound of leg of beef without bones cut into squares of about an inch; and two middling-sized onions, peeled and sliced; I then set the saucepan over a coal fire, and stirred the contents round for a few minutes with a wooden (or iron) spoon until fried lightly brown. I had then ready washed the peelings of two turnips, fifteen green leaves or tops of celery, and the green part of two leeks; (the whole of which, I must observe, are always thrown away). Having cut the above vegetables into small pieces, I threw them into the saucepan with

the other ingredients, stirring them occasionally over the fire for another ten minutes; then added one quart of cold water and three quarters of a pound of common flour and half a pound of pearl barley, mixing all well together; I then added seven quarts of hot water, seasoned with three ounces of salt, and a quarter of an ounce of brown sugar, stirred occasionally until boiling, and allowed to simmer very gently for three hours; at the end of which time I found the barley perfectly tender… The above soup has been tasted by numerous noblemen, members of parliament, and several ladies who have lately visited my kitchen department and who have considered it very good and nourishing … As regards the peelings and ends of vegetables which I use in my receipts, it is a well-known fact that the exteriors of every vegetable, roots in particular, contains more flavour than the interior of it … It will be perceived that I have omitted all kinds of spice except in those dishes which are intended expressly for them, as I consider they only flatter the appetite and irritate the stomach and make it crave for more food; my object being not to create an appetite but to satisfy it.'

Alexis Soyer: *Soyer's Charitable Cookery or the Poor Man's Regenerator*

Other root vegetables, such as carrots, can also be used and a thicker, more stew-like dish is created with less water.

TEA-CUP BREAD PUDDING

Even before Soyer, Francatelli wrote a cookery book 'for the working classes', which like most similar ones mixed good ideas and unpractical nonsense. This comes from the section of sick room recipes.

'Bruise a piece of stale crumb of bread the size of an egg, in a basin, add four lumps of sugar and a very little grated nutmeg, pour half a gill of boiling milk upon these, stir all well together until the sugar is melted, then add an egg, beat up the whole thoroughly until well mixed; pour the mixture into a buttered teacup, tie up in a small cloth ... [Francatelli's instructions here become rather muddled] ... boil the pudding for twenty minutes, at least, and as soon as done, turn it out on a plate. This, or any similar light kind of pudding, constitutes safe food for the most delicate.'

Charles Elmé Francatelli:
A Plain Cookery Book for the Working Classes

'It is not worth the while to live by rich cookery.'

Henry David Thoreau (1817–62)

History

COOKING METHODS AND TOOLS

A cook's working methods and tools are dictated by the kind of heat she uses, and how it is contained. In a poor home at the beginning of the 19th century, the fire was still set on a raised slab in the ground against a wall, and was fuelled by wood, peat or furze. A cauldron, pot or kettle (the name varied from place to place) hung by an iron chain (or rod with hook attached) from a bar in the chimney, or might be perched on the fire with its three stubby legs. This container was used for boiling stirabout (plain or flavoured porridge) or whatever else the family might have.

The poor housewife did not fry or broil (cook on a griddle) for lack of fat. Roasting, if done at all, was primitive. The meat might hang from the pot hook or be suspended by a piece of worsted from the front of the fireplace mantel, with a dish under it for the drips.

Some oatcakes or small loaves might be baked on the hearth on a flat hot bakestone, perhaps under an upturned crock or in a dry pot placed in the hot ashes. A beehive-shaped portable earthenware oven was sometimes used, covered with embers. But anyone in the country who had time or money for it sent their dough or pies to the communal village oven to be baked. City cookshops and bakers would roast or bake items for a small charge.

In a more affluent home, the fire was in a grate and fuelled by coal. Boiling was done in cast-iron pots like the ones in cottages, raised and lowered by a ratchet or a chimney crane. But roasting was a much more elaborate procedure in which the meat or bird was rotated in front of the fire over a drip-tray. Spits and the mechanisms for turning them were like those in the 18th century and remained almost unchanged, except for extra decoration, until the 1880s.

One development at the beginning of the 19th century, however, was to place the meat in a concave iron or tinplate 'reflector oven' like a screen, with the concave side open to the fire to reflect the heat on to the food. A door in the screen allowed access to the food from the back in order to baste it. Later, smaller similar roasters were developed with shelves for baking batch cakes or spikes for holding apples or bread for toasting.

Another 19th-century development was a clockwork bottle jack for turning the spit which did not depend on the heat of the fire to turn it.

Spit-roasting survived even after gas ovens came in. Oven-cooked meat, according to a cookbook editor in 1886, did not have the same flavour.

Broiled meat however was popular. Chops could be broiled, or pancakes fried, over the open fire in a cast-iron frying pan or on a gridiron (griddle) with a long handle.

The cast–iron open range, like cast iron itself and tinplate, had been developed in the late 18th century. By about 1830 it was commonplace in upper- and middle-class kitchens and in many solidly built smaller homes, because it could easily be built into an

Roasting over a spit

existing fireplace. The fire was still open for roasting and toasting, but had a cast-iron oven on one side. Early models had a swinging trivet at the other side to hold a kettle, and the grate could be made smaller by winding in the side or by folding down the top bars. In later models of this 'Yorkshire' range, as it was called, a set of hinged bars might fold down over the fire to support pots and pans, and by the 1860s a hot-water boiler was generally installed on the side opposite the oven.

In February 1802, George Bodley, a Devonshire iron-founder, had patented a closed-top range.

The range was the focal point of the Victorian kitchen

The design of this 'Kitchener' range was much like that of the Yorkshire type, but it had a cast-iron hotplate over the fire with removable boiling rings. The front of the fire could often be enclosed too by movable panels or a door, to redirect the heat for boiling or baking instead of roasting.

This combination stove became popular in affluent homes in southern England, because the cook could boil, fry and bake at the same time. But it was expensive to buy, very hard work to keep clean and a glutton for fuel. North country people stuck to the open range. (Poor people everywhere still cooked on a small open grate by balancing a kettle, frying pan or saucepan on the top.)

Experimental gas cookers and grills were tried out from 1824 onwards but did not become popular until the 1880s

Left: The Charing Cross Kitchener, 1890, an early example of a gas cooker.

Opposite: The kitchen at Brodsworth Hall in the Victorian period

in spite of promotion by enthusiasts. However, the experiments led to the development of gas cookers very similar to those of today and so, when the gas companies decided to promote them in the 1880s they had an efficient product to offer available in a range of

sizes and shapes. Vitreous enamel, wipe-down surfaces replaced the old black-leading needed for iron stoves. Well-insulated ovens with see-through doors made baking easier, although the temperature still had to be guessed. One new development was the grill which toasted food placed under it. It replaced the old gridirons on which food was broiled over the heat.

Penny-in-the-slot gas meters let even relatively poor people use gas. They could also hire gas cookers quite cheaply. By 1898, one home in four that had a gas supply, had a cooker as well.

The first electric power station for domestic consumers did not open until the 1880s, and although electric cookers were being demonstrated in the 1890s along with other electrical cooking equipment, their history really belongs to the 20th century.

The development of the closed cast-iron cooking range changed the shape of cooking pots and pans. They now needed to be flat-bottomed and no longer

Blacking for the kitchen range

Opposite: Cast-iron and copper pots and pans

needed long handles. They also got smaller because the range could hold more of them, and as fancy cooking became popular with the rising middle class, they became more specialised. A mid-Victorian cook might have, for instance, an omelette pan, a sauté pan, a frying pan, separate fish kettles for flat and round fish, and for salmon. Luckily for her, these were no longer made of copper or brass which needed hard scouring, but of tinplated cast iron varnished black. Towards the end of the century, vitreous enamel began to be used as a finish, and lightweight aluminium cookware first appeared.

Ladles, spoons, chopping knives, mashers, herb choppers and other traditional implements did not change, but a number of more specialised tools and gadgets were added to them, many of them metal versions of earlier ones. Mass-produced tinware flooded middle-class kitchens: for example, pastry and biscuit cutters, patty pans, pikelet rings and jelly moulds. A boiled tongue could be curled up and pressed in a tinplate screw-down press like a cheese-press. Tinplate biscuit and sweet tins, often gaudily painted, replaced bottles, jars and boxes. The essential tin-opener was introduced during the 1860s to open cans of corned beef.

Free-standing toasters of various shapes were elaborated for making some of the more delicate dishes eaten at formal dinners. A common type was a tripod with a multi-pronged attachment and a drip-tray beneath which could be used for cooking small birds, fruits, nuts or cheese, as well as for toasting bread.

After 1865, tinned cast-iron and tinplate were combined in many mechanical labour-saving gadgets. A grater, bread rasper, potato peeler, mincer, bean slicer, marmalade cutter, knife sharpener and an enormous complicated apple corer, peeler and slicer were just some of them. There was even a chopper and mixer – but no blender.

Ice had been cut in blocks and stored in underground or well-insulated ice-houses since 1660 and this supply, together with imported block ice from Norway and America, cooled late Georgian and Victorian food for parties. About 1840, tin or zinc-lined boxes came into use.

A knife grinder – an invaluable aid in a busy Victorian kitchen

They were packed with ice with the food on top. About fifteen years later, similar ice-chests were patented which had a top, aerated compartment for crushed ice, a drainage system for melted ice-water, and a lower chilled compartment for food. The prototype refrigerator, which it was called, had been created.

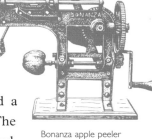

Bonanza apple peeler

The sorbets, ice-creams and iced puddings which had become immensely popular for formal upper- and rising middle-class dinners could not be frozen in a small quantity of crushed ice alone. Experiments in making artificial ice led to the discovery that ice mixed with salpetre or salt made a colder, longer-lasting freezing mixture. In about 1864, experiments in America showed that churning ice-cream while it froze improved its texture. Ice-cream makers or freezers were therefore developed which were like a box or pail with a cylinder inside which contained the flavoured cream and was cranked by a handle. In later models, a paddle inside the cream container was worked by turning a handle.

In fact, Victorian cookery was not unlike that of today – except that the cook still prepared her own meat, fowl and fish as well as kneading, mixing and whisking by hand. Her gadgets were still clumsier than her fingers.

Advertisement for a patent ice-cream maker – the actual model is illustrated on p36

34   *Advertisements.*

BY ROYAL LETTERS PATENT.

MARSHALL'S PATENT FREEZER.

Complete View.

IS PRAISED BY ALL WHO KNOW IT FOR

CHEAPNESS in first cost.   CLEANLINESS in working.
ECONOMY in use.   SIMPLICITY in construction.
RAPIDITY in freezing.

MENU

Caviar Sur Croûtes
Croûte au Pot
Saumon bouilli,
Sauce Écrivisses
Côtelettes de Pigeon
à l'Américaine
Poulet à la Valencienne
Pommes de Terre frites
Épinards à la Crème

Vict Pudding à la Mousselinade
Dessert and Ices

SERVICE, SETTINGS
AND MANNERS

To see how the new foodstuffs, materials and appliances changed the way people ate in the Victorian period, we must first focus on the meals of the people who used them – the rising middle class.

In the early Victorian period, breakfast was taken between 9 and 10am as in the 18th century, but it became more substantial. The aristocratic 18th-century custom of having just chocolate, coffee or tea, toast and hot sweet rolls still held for some people but a cooked breakfast was popular with men. Jane Austen mentions boiled eggs and pork chops.

Luncheon was still a light snack meal, and was taken at about 1 o'clock to fill the gap between breakfast and the new, but variable, later dinner hour. This was rapidly getting later because more and more men worked in their own, or other people's, offices. Jane Austen regarded 5 or 6pm as a reasonable dinner hour in 1805 with evening tea – an 18th-century introduction – two or three hours later and, for greedy entertaining, a late supper before bedtime.

Opposite: Fine china, burnished silver and engraved glasses provide an elegant place setting

A plain everyday dinner at home might consist of only three or four savoury dishes, with a couple of sweet dishes afterwards or perhaps cheese. But a formal dinner was still set out in 18th-century style in two or three courses or 'services' – in fact, two complete self-service meals were served, one after the other.

One new feature of such a dinner was that, although servants were at hand to change the plates and pour wine, gentlemen carved for and served their lady neighbours, and only from the dishes close by; it was not thought polite to stretch or demand a dish at the other end of the table.

Dishes and tableware had already in the 18th century begun to have the shapes we know now, but there were some novelties. For instance, early in the 19th century, it became fashionable to use silver servers, knives and forks for eating fish and fruit because it was thought that using steel spoiled the flavour, and that acid foods corroded the metal. More important, bone china with its translucent body and sparkling glaze was developed to beautify dinner tables.

Two cloths were laid on the table, one for removal between courses or before the dessert. (Table mats, leaving the table bare,

Tea-time with Spode china illustrated in a still life painting by George Foster, 1872

now began to be used at lunch but never at dinner.) In the centre of the tablecloth was placed a grand food dish, a plateau or an épergne. A plateau was a chased silver or glass oblong tray with rounded ends, on small feet. An épergne was a tall ornament, with branches which held small dishes of sweetmeats, fruit or flowers.

Later in the century, it would often be replaced by a flower arrangement or by a tazza – a stemmed shallow bowl or plate like a cake stand for fruit, sweetmeats or trailing floral decorations.

One marked change in dining habits occurred early on. Instead of the ladies entering the room first in order of precedence, followed by the gentlemen, so that the sexes were seated separately, it became the custom for each lady to be escorted into dinner by a gentleman, who then sat next to her. However, in spite of this 'promiscuous seating' as it was called, etiquette demanded that all the ladies should be served first as in the past; and from this grew the custom of every gentleman serving his lady companion before himself. He must then also (since a lady might not ask for wine) make sure that she was served, both during and after dinner, with the wine she preferred. He should call for the same wine for himself, and when the glasses came, bow to his companion and drink with her.

Separate styles of glasses were now beginning to be used for different wines. The number of wines served with a meal also increased. By the 1850s, a different wine would be served at each stage of the meal, each in a special glass, and these would be arrayed on the table beside each diner instead of being called for.

'Finger glasses' – the small glasses of water supplied before the dessert for rinsing out the mouth – were used for a different purpose in Victorian times. Early in the 19th century they began

to be used instead to wet the corner of the napkin to wipe the mouth and then to rinse the fingertips.

There were not many other refinements yet. Men still stayed drinking in the dining room long after dinner, and their manners were as coarse as in the 18th century. Ladies stayed only after the dessert for perhaps two glasses of wine, and then retired.

In the second half of the 19th century, three important changes took place in Victorian well-to-do eating patterns:

> '**One can say everything best over a meal.**'
>
> George Eliot
> (Mary Ann Evans) (1819–80)

mealtimes changed, meals became larger and more elaborate, and the serving system changed completely.

As the pattern of 'going to the office' developed, breakfast got slightly earlier and dinner a lot later. A man might go to his club after his office day, before returning home to change his clothes and have one of the newly popular aperitifs; so dinner seldom took place before 8, 9 or 10pm if entertaining.

The Victorian breakfast was a hearty affair. Mrs Beeton in 1861 suggested any cold joint in the larder might be placed 'nicely garnished' on the sideboard along with the collared and potted meats or fish, cold game or poultry, veal and ham pies, game pies, cold ham and tongue – pressed in the new style tin press. These were to supplement a choice of hot dishes, such as broiled mackerel or other fish, mutton chops and rump steaks, broiled sheeps' kidneys, sausages (now prepared and sold by butchers), bacon and eggs, other kinds of eggs, muffins, toast, marmalade, butter, jam, tea and coffee. She suggested adding fruit in the summer.

Lunch was still quite light. The same cold dishes would do as at breakfast, or a mother might eat the same hot meal as the children. If a woman entertained, the dishes would be dainty rather than filling, but this was not common, and she was more likely to have soup, or chicken sandwiches alone. However, if it was her At Home Day, she would serve a new meal of afternoon tea with hot teacakes, thin sandwiches and an array of small cakes and biscuits, and at least one large cake made with baking powder instead of yeast.

And then there was dinner. The quantity which well-to-do Victorians served and ate at a dinner party was prodigious. Even a small dinner for six given by people of modest means in 1861 contained at least thirteen dishes and dessert. A wealthier dinner later in the century was a lot more lavish. However, Mrs Beeton,

Opposite: Detail from *Dinner at Haddo House* by Alfred Edward Emslie, 1884

alongside these meals, suggests menus for Plain Family Dinners such as bubble and squeak made from the remains of cold beef, and curried pork followed by baked semolina pudding.

Copying French custom, a new way of serving meals had begun to creep in during the early 1800s, but it was not really adopted in middle-class homes until the 1850s, and even then Mrs Beeton was dubious about it. More staff were needed to serve it, and more cutlery to eat it with.

The new style consisted of sending to table one kind of dish at a time, beginning with soup and fish, then made-up meat dishes (entrées), roasts, poultry and game, then vegetable and sweet dishes called entremets, and finally desserts.

Fashionable dining also demanded that all the serving

Helping the cook with the Sunday roast

(including carving) be done in the kitchen so that diners were issued with a ready-prepared plate.

English hostesses wavered but finally, towards the end of the 19th century, settled for a compromise in which modern-style courses (soup, fish, etc) were sent to the table in turn, any carving was done at a side table, and the dish, or choice of dishes, was handed round to the diners.

What made such a dinner so very different from today was that there were usually six or seven courses and a choice – sometimes a wide choice – in each. At a really long, large dinner, the cook might also serve an iced sorbet after the main course to revive the palate.

It was as well that dishes were now handed round because there was no room for them on the table among the clutter of assorted wine glasses, rows of knives and forks, tasse, vases of flowers and napkins twisted into fancy shapes. All these were larger than before and more elaborate. The Victorians engraved, embossed, curled and chased every surface. Curiously, they standardised the shapes of cutlery, such as knife-blades and the tines of forks. The development of EPNS (electroplated nickel silver)

A Victorian method of making a table napkin look decorative

The Mitre

Fold the napkin in three, lengthways

Fold the ends to the middle

Fold over the top corners

Turn the folded napkin over, raise the outer corners and tuck into each other to form the finished mitre design

90

The Collegian

Fold the napkin in four, lengthways

Turn down the ends diagonally from the centre

Turn the folded napkin over and roll up the ends

Turn the rolls under as indicated by the diagonal dotted lines shown above

The Victorian table napkin was a 30 inch square of starched and crisply ironed linen damask, which was folded into a variety of ornamental forms and set beside each place setting on the dining table

tableware for modest homes in the latter part of the period encouraged this.

No mid-Victorian table would have been complete without a vase of flowers. Mrs Beeton even stresses that one should be placed on the breakfast table. At dinner parties, the height of the flower arrangements tended to make conversation impossible across the table. However, this hardly mattered since good manners demanded that polite conversation should be confined to one's neighbours.

By the 1850s, table manners had become genteel. Fish, for instance, should be eaten with just a fork and a scrap of bread – one should only toy with one's silver (or EPNS) fish knife. One should eat only a little of each dish, and that delicately. It was no longer 'done' to wet one's napkin to dab the mouth; ladies especially, should dabble only the fingertips in the finger-bowl. It was not done either, to gulp down a glass of wine. Even gentlemen drank slowly of the different wines served with each course, until the ladies left the room and they could settle to their port; and even then they were expected to appear in the drawing room quite soon after the ladies' coffee-tray had been removed.

Between dinner parties, the average, reasonably affluent Victorian family lived relatively plainly. Nevertheless, by modern standards, they spent a disproportionate amount of their time thinking about food and drink, and in entertaining for show. A well-to-do married couple with business connections might give four dinner parties a month, for 12–16 guests each, and serve 20–30 dishes each time, at considerable cost. It was fortunate that their cook now would have had a mincer, bean slicer, bread rasper, wire egg whisk, packet jellies, custard powder, ice-box, freezer pail and above all her combination Kitchener to produce the showy dishes on the sparkling plate which these occasions required.

Victorian values – home, friendship and above all a good meal, by Charles Meer Webb, 1883

BIBLIOGRAPHY

Brett, Gerard, *Dinner is Served*, Rupert Hart Davis (London, 1968).

Brooke, Sheena, *Hearth and Home: a short history of domestic equipment in England*, Mills & Boon (London, 1973).

Burnett, John (ed), *Useful Toil*, Allen Lane (Harmondsworth, 1974).

Burton, Elizabeth, *The Early Victorians at Home*, Arrow Books (London, 1972).

Currah, Anne (ed), *Chef to Queen Victoria: the recipes of Charles Elmé Francatelli*, William Kimber (London, 1973).

Davidson, Caroline, *A Woman's Work is Never Done*, Chatto & Windus (London, 1982).

Davis, Michael Justin (ed), *In a Wiltshire Village: scenes from rural Victorian life*, Alan Sutton (Stroud, 1981).

Drummond, J C, and Wilbraham, A, *The Englishman's Food*, Jonathan Cape (London, 1969).

Feild, Rachael, *Irons in the Fire*, Crowood Press (Marlborough, 1984).

Hickman, Peggy, *A Jane Austen Household Book with Martha Lloyd's Recipes*, David & Charles (Newton Abbot, 1977).

Margetson, Stella, *Leisure and Pleasure in the Nineteenth Century*, Cassell (London, 1969).

Norwak, Mary, *Kitchen Antiques*, Ward Lock (London, 1975).

Recipe Books

Acton, Eliza, *Modern Cookery for Private Families*, Longmans Green, Reader and Dyer, 1855; facsimile edition by Elek Press (London, 1966).

Beeton, Isabella (ed), *The Book of Household Management*, Ward Lock and Tyler, 1861; facsimile edition by Jonathan Cape (London, 1968).

Black, Mrs, *Superior Cookery*, William Collins, Sons & Co (Glasgow, c1898).

Francatelli, Charles Elmé, *A Plain Cookery Book for the Working Classes*, 1852; reprinted by Scolar Press (London, 1977).

— *The Cook's Guide and Housekeeper's and Butler's Assistant*, Richard Bentley & Son (1877).

Bibliography

Gordon, Martha H, *Cookery for Working Men's Wives*, Alexander Gardner (1888).

Hobbs, Samuel, *One Hundred and Sixty Culinary Dainties for the Epicure, the Invalid and the Dyspeptic*, Dean & Son (c1890).

Kitchiner, William MD, *The Cook's Oracle*, (1817).

Senn, Charles Herman, *Recherché Cookery and Practical Gastronomy and Culinary Dictionary*, Spottiswoode and Co (London, 1895).

Soyer, Alexis, *The Modern Housewife or Ménagère* and *Soyer's Charitable Cookery or the Poor Man's Regenerator*, Simkin, Marshall and Co (1853).

Wentworth, J (ed), *Janey Ellice's Recipes 1846–1859*, Macdonald and Jane's (London, 1975).

ACKNOWLEDGEMENTS

The publishers would like to thank Janet Tattersley, Rob Richardson and Val Horsler for cooking and presenting a number of recipes featured in this book and James O Davies and Peter Williams for photographing them. They are also grateful to Maggie Scrivens for her help in the preparation of this book.

The publishers would like to thank Brodsworth Hall, Yorkshire, for giving us permission to use photographs from their collection, and the following people and organisations listed below for permission to reproduce the photographs in this book. Every care has been taken to trace copyright holders, but any omissions will, if notified, be corrected in any future edition.

All photographs are © English Heritage or © Crown copyright.NMR with the exception of the following: Front cover: Fine Art Photographic Library/Gallery Mensing; pp8, 20 Derry Brabbs; pp 12, 17, 21, 48, 57 Mary Evans Picture Library; p39 London Library, St James's Square, London, UK/courtesy of The Bridgeman Art Library; pp49, 87 National Portrait Gallery; p81 Christie's Images; p92 Phillips, The International Fine Art Auctioneers/courtesy of The Bridgeman Art Library.

RECIPE INDEX

Other titles in this series:
Roman Cookery
Medieval Cookery
Tudor Cookery
Stuart Cookery
Georgian Cookery
Ration Book Cookery